Abhijit Naskar is the twenty-first century Neuroscientist whose contributions in Cognitive and Behavioral Neuroscience have helped the world tackle the issues of mental illness, prejudice, hate, extremism, discrimination and segregation more effectively. As an untiring advocate of mental health and universal acceptance, he became a beloved best-selling author all over the world with his very first book "The Art of Neuroscience in Everything". With his pioneering ventures into the Neuropsychology of beliefs and biases, he has hugely contributed in the eradication of religious and cultural differences in our world, for which he is popularly hailed as a humanitarian scientist, who takes the human civilization in the path of sweet general harmony.

ain't ENOUGH *to look* HUMAN

ABHIJIT NASKAR

Also by Abhijit Naskar

The Art of Neuroscience in Everything
Your Own Neuron: A Tour of Your Psychic Brain
The God Parasite: Revelation of Neuroscience
The Spirituality Engine
Love Sutra: The Neuroscientific Manual of Love
Homo: A Brief History of Consciousness
Neurosutra: The Abhijit Naskar Collection
Autobiography of God: Biopsy of A Cognitive Reality
Biopsy of Religions: Neuroanalysis towards Universal
Tolerance
Prescription: Treating India's Soul
What is Mind?
In Search of Divinity: Journey to The Kingdom of Conscience
Love, God & Neurons: Memoir of a scientist who found
himself by getting lost
The Islamophobic Civilization: Voyage of Acceptance
Neurons of Jesus: Mind of A Teacher, Spouse & Thinker
Neurons, Oxygen & Nanak
The Education Decree
Principia Humanitas
The Krishna Cancer
Rowdy Buddha: The First Sapiens
We Are All Black: A Treatise on Racism
The Bengal Tigress: A Treatise on Gender Equality
Either Civilized or Phobic: A Treatise on Homosexuality
Wise Mating: A Treatise on Monogamy
Illusion of Religion: A Treatise on Religious
Fundamentalism
The Film Testament
Human Making is Our Mission: A Treatise on Parenting
I Am The Thread: My Mission
7 Billion Gods: Humans Above All
Lord is My Sheep: Gospel of Human
Morality Absolute
A Push in Perception
Let The Poor Be Your God
Conscience over Nonsense
Saint of The Sapiens
Time to Save Medicine
Fabric of Humanity

Build Bridges not Walls: In the name of Americana
The Constitution of The United Peoples of Earth
Lives to Serve Before I Sleep
When Humans Unite: Making A World Without Borders
All For Acceptance
Monk Meets World
Mission Reality
Citizens of Peace: Beyond The Savagery of Sovereignty
Operation Justice: To Make A Society That Needs No Law
See No Gender
The Gospel of Technology
Every Generation Needs Caretakers: The Gospel of
Patriotism
Aşkanjali: The Sufi Sermon
Mad About Humans: World Maker's Almanac
Revolution Indomable
When Call The People: My World My Responsibility
No Foreigner Only Family
Hurricane Humans: Give me accountability, I'll give you
peace

This book is dedicated to all the honest, hardworking small business owners who are the lifeblood of local economy

CONTENTS

1. Humanity A to Z (The Poem)

Humanity A to Z
(The Poem)

A for assimilation is the way,
B for bigotry must be thrown away.
C for conscience when at play,
D for delusions all run away.
E for equality once brought to life,
F for fears can no longer survive.
G for greed when let not to thrive,
H for humility won't be caught in strife.
I for integrity mustn't be compromised,
J for justice will then prevail alright.
K for kindness must never run tight,
L for life can then be lived upright.
M for mercy can never be forgotten,
N for naivety keeps you from being rotten.
O for oppression when is begotten,
P for patience must be overridden.
Q for questions when let fly,
R for rigidity will weaken and die.
S for serenity will go awry,
T for tradition if obeyed dry.
U for unity is our supreme mission,
V for vanity leads only to destruction.
W for wholeness is our salvation,
X for xenophobia is no civilization.

Y for yield we must never to separation,
Z for zeal we mustn't lose for ascension.

2. When Bones Ignite

People ask me, you are a scientist, why do you write on politics? I tell them, I don't write on politics, I am a scientist of human nature, so I write on human nature, and so long as politics has humans in it, my work will involve politics as well along with all other sectors of the society that are run by humans. In short, my work is on human welfare. And to be actively involved in human welfare is not politics, it's humanity. Politics is merely a tiny part of it all, nothing more.

Humanity is a word without bounds, in fact, it can't be bound by words - it can't be bound by ideologies - it can't be bound by opinions and beliefs - humanity extends beyond any one person's wildest imagination. Humanity is not constant, it is ever-evolving. Humanity is the force of becoming more human and less animal. And this force continues to work through those who are willing. It makes them grow - it makes them learn - it makes them aware - it makes them live - live not as mere animal, but as a being of conscience and character.

Humanity is not something you compromise - yet we do. Humanity is not something you take for granted - yet we do. Humanity is not something you deem secondary - yet we do. As a result, it's a world of humans alright, but not of humanity - not yet anyways. Only when there's humanity in you, you are worthy of the title human.

The title human is not our birthright, we have to earn it by living with humanity. If we do not, then we are to be counted among the animals, not humans. Sometimes I wonder, how many of the seven billion humans are actually humans! The arrogant and the shallow may shout with utter pride, who's going to judge who's human and who's not! Nobody - nobody is going to judge nobody - however, if you are more worried about being judged, than being concerned with being human, then you have already proven yourself to be a non-human. Isn't it so my friend! Think.

When humanity is at play in you, there is no insecurity of being judged, for a true human is too involved in human welfare to be insecure. When you work for the people, you have only one concern in your mind, to lift the people - no matter what, the people must be lifted. If we don't give back to the society, we'll die of obesity.

When your bones ignite and your blood boils at the sight of misery, injustice and hate, that's when you are truly born as a human. However, the unfortunate reality of the society is that, this human is never born in most of the human population for whatever reason - in some it's due to insecurity and fear - in some it's due to prejudice - in some others it's due to indifference. Whatever the reason may be, most humans rarely live as humans, because living is so precious to them that they forget to consider whether that living has life in it.

Remember, a brave death is far better than a cowardly life. Now the question is why - why do so many people on earth live with cowardice instead of bravery! And the answer is, that's how all of us are raised - none of us are raised to be thinkers or leaders or revolutionaries - we are all raised to take our loyal place in society - loyal to the norms - loyal to the traditions. In short, we are all raised as slaves of society - and that's where all the trouble begins - with our innate slavery. So, if you want things to change, take a stand and rise not as slavehearts but bravehearts.

3. Beyond The Slavery of Society

Hard as it may sound, injustice, inequality and bigotry will prevail in the society for a long time, and that is more reason for you to prepare the mental grounds of your children, so that they could stand up to the inhumanities of the world with a bold heart and high head.

It pleases me to tell you that, through rigorous revolutions from people across cultures, we have succeeded in diminishing slavery to a great extent, and the traces that remain in the form of systemic racism, will soon turn powerless with our continuous fight against it. Having said that, now is the time that you raise leaders not just in your children, but also in yourself. Enough of this slave's existence, now is the time you break free and redeem your soul from the archaic clutches of society.

There is a difference between servant of society and slave of society. The slaves of society live their life exactly like the masses, without giving a single thought to the implications of such a life, whereas the servant of society works to benefit the society even if it means going against the accepted norms of the society.

Norms indicate the normal way of life, but the normal way of life is not necessarily the right way of life. In fact, in most cases of the so-called civilized society, the normal way of life is the wrong of life. Let me tell you why. And for that let's take a look at the normal way of life. The normal way of life is predicated greatly on the obsession over the needs of the self. And no society can progress with self-obsession as its usual lifestyle.

Without a sense of community - without a genuine concern for the society - a concern that is uninfluenced, uncorrupted, unconditioned, it's not a civilized society to begin with, let alone be a progressive society. Society can progress only if its people feel responsible. And by being responsible I am not talking about following norms mark you - being responsible of one's society means doing what's best not just for oneself alone, but for the entire community.

This has nothing to do with the popular concept of being different, for such a term is merely a plaything in the hands of self-obsessed people, young and old alike. Let me tell you how. A great many people confuse attention with admiration, they think a stunt is an achievement and misbehavior a declaration of independence. So to such self-obsessed bunch, being different is just about being different, it has no further influence in the society whatsoever, beyond the disorder it creates with its utter recklessness.

4. Gospel of Boldness

Recklessness is not a sign of boldness, it's only a sign of primitiveness. If you want to be truly bold, then come out of your narrow lanes of self-obsession and place yourself at the feet of the helpless and the destitute, only then can you be rightfully called bold, and more importantly only then can you be truly called a human.

Recklessness, callousness, apathy - these are signs of descension, not ascension. So, what are the opposites of recklessness, callousness and apathy - it's only one simple word - accountability. Accountability brings out the best in us, whereas recklessness brings out the worst in us. When we are accountable, we are a vessel of goodness - we are the very force for good.

However, if you do a few good deeds and then say, that's it, I've completed my daily quota of good deeds, then that's not goodness, but a mockery of goodness. When a river flows does it ever count the villages it passes by and then say that's it, I have completed my daily quota of providing people water - it doesn't, it simply keeps flowing, without keeping count of how many people are blessed by its water. Be like the river my friend and do good without keeping count.

And do good not because good things will happen to you if you do good - in fact, even if you do good, good things may not happen, but do good anyways, because goodness is the highest use of human life. Read a few books, you live a little, but help a few people, you live a lifetime. Life mustn't be measured by time, but by goodness. To put it simply, if you are doing good in your ordinary everyday life, then only you are living, or else, you are wasting your lifeforce in an illusion of life.

Your faith, your nationality, your profession, your societal status, your ancestry - all these have no bearing on your goodness. That's why, I don't care about your religious belief or disbelief, I don't care about your intellect, I don't care about your bank balance, all I care about is your behavior with others. The size of a human heart cannot be measured by money, ancestry or popularity, it can only be measured by love - by kindness - by compassion. Call it whatever you may, it's all one and the same. The heart of a society must be big enough to fill its chest. If it's not, it's no human heart in the first place, but a heart of the lowest of animals.

5. Matter of Heart

What is a heart - is it merely an organ pumping blood through our body, or is it something more? And the answer is both. When we are talking about physiology, heart is merely an organ pumping blood, nothing more than that - this organ holds no feelings whatsoever. But when we are talking about psychology, the term heart has a much deeper significance, way beyond its physiological counterpart. Heart is a symposium of human emotions, civilized emotions that is, not the primitive ones - and this psychological heart lives not in the bloodpump inside your chest, but in the brain inside your skull.

Everything that makes us human is born in the brain, just like everything that makes us animal is also born in the brain - it's only our determination that makes one dominant over the other. But here the important fact to keep in mind is that, the animal parts of us do not need our special attention to be dominant, in fact, in the absence of our determination to be human, the animal in us automatically takes over.

So, if we really, truly, genuinely want to turn an animal world into a human society, we must be absolutely human first. But being absolutely human doesn't mean that the animal in us stops existing, it only means that we have made our determination of humanhood so strong that the animal doesn't stand a chance, so it is compelled to relinquish command of the psyche. But the moment you let your guard down, it wakes up and takes control instantly, thus turning you into an animal in human clothing.

So, be aware at all times - and be determined to be human. Because it's not enough that you look human, for the animal inside of you has been there for billions of years. So, never ever relinquish command of your psyche. It's a human psyche only when the human is awake (not to confuse with literal sleep and wakefulness).

You must wake up the human in you first to make this world human. A human world is a civilized world - not one that's human by appearance only, but one that's human by thought, feeling and action. And that world starts with you - as a matter of fact, it starts with you and ends with you.

This means that, only if you are human by thought, feeling and action, can the world be human - only then can the world be humane. The very reason for the birth of the word humane is that the term human has failed so far to depict the true qualities of a civilized being of conscience and character. What this means is that, the world knows there are animals among the humans, but they are too shallow or insecure to point them out as such, in the name of civility. Hence, they use the term human to refer to the entirety of the human population, including the human looking animals, such as racists, bigots and fundamentalists, and the term humane to refer to the true civilized qualities of a creature of conscience and character.

Now, there is nothing wrong with using different terms to refer to humanity, but what's wrong is the innate indifference to inhumanity. And indifference has been pompously labeled as civility. In short, civility is the fake nicety that people ought to exchange, even while greeting an obvious animal. And such a behavior has only made the society more shallow.

6. Accountability over Law

A functional society is full of norms. There are norms that you ought to follow, then there are norms that you must follow. Those that you ought to follow are usually sustained in the population through habit, and those that you must follow are enforced by law. The very purpose of law is to hold people accountable - it is the ultimate tool for the authorities of the society to maintain order. But here is the interesting part, the presence of law implies not the presence of order, but the presence of disorder.

If you are accountable - if you don't do anything wrong - then you need not bother with law. You are only bound by law, when you intend to do something wrong. I am not bound by law, for my law is my accountability towards society, which itself makes me do what's right and best for the society. I am not here to be guided by the illusive societal paradigms, legal or any other, I am here to point those paradigms in a humane direction, so that they can recognize their shortcomings and evolve into something better. But if ever the dark day comes when I commit an inhumanity, I will sentence myself to death.

But again, the very parameters of right and wrong in the domain of law vary from nation to nation, based on the ethical state and understanding of the people of each nation. Which means, what's right in one nation, may be wrong in another nation, and vise-versa. And when this is the case, how can any law ever claim to have any true understanding of right and wrong in the first place.

That's why new legislation takes place regularly, so that what is considered right today, if it's observed to be actually wrong or unfit for the current time and age, then it can be declared wrong tomorrow - or what is considered wrong today, if it actually is observed to be right, that is, if the evidence against it turns out to be baseless in the new time and age, then it can be declared right tomorrow.

In this context, the most glaring example that comes to mind is gay marriage. Gay marriage which was once considered blasphemy, hence illegal, after careful conscientious consideration, is now being legalized across the planet. And I went into this matter thoroughly in my treatise on homosexuality entitled "Either Civilized or Phobic", whence came my statement – *"love has no gender, compassion has no religion, character has no race."*

Like all other fields, law is not perfect, but so long as it doesn't stop scrutinizing itself in an attempt to correct its errors, it will keep serving as a quintessential part of the societal architecture. However, as I said, law is not perfect - and it will not be for a long time, perhaps never - so, in the meantime, if you fall prey to the imperfections of the law, that is, if you ever find yourself in a position where you are wrongfully accused by the law, don't despair and don't act on impulse either - bring all your conscience and wit to action. Remember, no matter the nation, law always has loopholes, and if you are driven and witty enough, you can use them to your advantage. That's how many guilty criminals get acquitted in the first place, that is, by abusing the loopholes of law.

Law is healthy so long as it's intended to empower the right, but the moment it tries to control a population driven by its own biases, prejudice and rigidity, it is the responsibility of the people to come together and disavow such law. Law is to serve the people, not control them, if it does, the people as caring guardians must give it a nice spanking by means of a revolution.

Law and justice do not always go hand in hand, and in those times, more than any other time, the responsibility to sustain justice in society falls on the shoulders of the people. People are the alpha - people are the omega - no law, science, art and religion should ever forget that. Law exists so long as it has the consent of the people - science exists so long as it has the consent of the people - art exists so long as it has the consent of the people - religion exists so long as it has the consent of the people.

All of these exist so long as they have the best interest of the people in mind. Even to lead the people you need their consent and you do not get that consent by asking to lead, you get that by serving without being asked. Service is the highway to salvation. To serve is to lead - to serve is to breathe - to serve is to live. And such a life is the highest proof of humanity. Try not to count on the humanity of others, present yourself as the proof of humanity. Offer yourself as a living flag - the flag of a people - not the flag of a nation or religion or ideology – but the supreme flag of a species - of our species - the flag of humankind.

There is darkness in our world, but that darkness won't go away if you simply sit down on your couch and pray, or attend Sunday communions and sing hymns - that darkness can only be eliminated if you turn yourself into a flame of light, just like Jesus did for the poor and oppressed. Christ did his humane duty when he was alive, so did Buddha, Nanak, Rumi and many more, I am doing mine - and now it's your turn. Turn yourself into a living Christ, only then can there be hope for the upliftment of the world.

7. Makers of Reality

Space and time are usually separate from thought, but the moment you build the bridge of action, they all become intertwined and what you think manifests into reality. There is no magic involved. It's this simple, thought creates reality but only through action. Let me give you an example. You can sit in a dark room and think of light all you want, but that won't change the reality of the darkness around, but step up to light a candle and suddenly the dark reality turns into one filled with light.

Reality is in your hand - not just that - reality is your responsibility, because the reality you create with your action or inaction will essentially be the reality that you will hand over to your children. So to hand over a humane reality, be the very definition of humanity in front of your children and leave the rest to nature. Church visits and prayers are okay as a healthy practice of self-preservation, if you can do them without building a wall between you and the people from other belief systems, but they are absolutely worthless if in your everyday life you don't step up and act as a human.

To put it simply, prayer or no prayer, step up and act. Remember, one real toddler is capable of more change than a thousand imaginary gods. Without action, no prayer can bring change - without motion, no hymn can bring change. Stagnant water never achieves anything, it neither quenches someone's thirst nor does it help grow a plant, it only breeds disease.

To achieve anything in life you actually have to throw away your rigidity and act, or else, you exist as a mockery of life, as a living disease on earth. Add life to this world my friend, not disease. Remember, diseases of the psyche, such as bigotry, prejudice, racism, fundamentalism and arrogance, which are still unrecorded by the clinical community, do more harm to the self and the society than the obvious recorded mental disorders.

A progressive society is a self-scrutinizing society. But mark you, I am not talking about being judgmental, rather I am talking about paying attention to your strongholds as well as your shortcomings, for only when you pay attention will you be able to observe - observe what you are good at - observe what you are bad at - observe what your errors are - observe where your potential lies.

You know what a being of character is - one who is never afraid to acknowledge their mistakes. Be aware of your mistakes, be aware of our ancestors' mistakes, be aware of the mistakes of others and apply what you learn in your own life, not just to correct your mistakes, but more importantly to become more human. There is not and there never will be an absolute human, for a true human is always evolving - a true human is always growing - and as we grow at our own free will, the world will keep getting a bit more humane.

The moment we stop growing is the moment we become a disease on earth. And this growth includes everything that we consider part of human life and society - there is no exception, not traditions, not gods, deities and messiahs, not holy books, not religion, not beliefs, not cultural tenets, not national characteristics, not the constitution, nothing. Everything that makes us who we are, must grow, it must evolve, discarding the shortcomings and embracing the strengths.

8. The Battle Within

Evolution is predicated on action, inaction leads to extinction. But this is not as simple as it sounds. Let's get into the gravitas of the matter. Just imagine, not a single species on earth has ever been able to influence the direction of their own evolution - that is, until now. And this is nothing to be taken lightly. We may not yet be independent of nature, but we are no longer completely at the mercy of nature either unlike all the other species on earth. We may not be stronger than nature, but we are not weak either, not any more that is. We have developed mental capacities unimaginable by any other species, and these capacities have rendered physical strength irrelevant, except in sports.

But the question is, are we aware of our own capacities and if we are, do we at all put those capacities to good use! So far we have been behaving like a superhero who uses his or her power not to help people, but for personal gain. I know this is a childish example, but sometimes the only way to see the right from the wrong is to look from a child's perspective. And as a matter of fact, compared to all other animals we humans are indeed like superheroes.

No one creature can develop the unique faculties of another creature. For example, a fish's unique faculty is to breathe under water, but a bird cannot do that, and on the other hand, a bird's unique faculty is flight, which a fish can never accomplish (of course there are certain species that can do both, but even those creatures cannot develop faculties of all other creatures).

But when it comes to humans, things get extremely intriguing. By the grace of the most advanced mind on earth, we humans can develop perfect substitutes for the faculties of almost all the creatures on earth - we can fly like a bird through airplanes - we can swim under water like a fish through oxygen tanks - we can see in the dark like a fox through night vision goggles or just a plain flashlight - we can run fast like a cheetah through motorcycles and automobiles - the list just goes on.

However, these are all external feats of achievement, which we have mastered quite well, but when it comes to mastering the world inside of us, things get rather primitive. It's true that we have extraordinary and unparalleled mental capacities, but the other side of the story is that we also possess the primitive instincts that drive the very lives of the animals in the wild. So, every moment there goes a battle between civilization and savagery inside of us.

And the only way that your civilized side can win is if you practice self-regulation, humility and simplicity as a way of living. The more you practice the more it becomes natural for you. Eventually your mind develops an automatic, that is, subconscious faculty to keep the primitive side in check. However, you will still need to keep your powers of observation wide open, so that prejudice, bias or any other kind of savagery is never expressed through your behavior.

Now here what I must mention is that I am no idealist, I am a biologist, which means that I know what we humans are and what we are capable of, so I won't say that with observation you'll always be successful in avoiding a savagery, but even if you do commit a savagery due to whatever reason, make sure to observe and acknowledge it so that it doesn't happen twice. But if you keep repeating such savageries despite being observant, seek medical help immediately, for there may be a pathological reason behind your savagery and not just plain old primitive instincts.

9. Fundamentals of Progress

Observation breeds understanding and action upon that understanding breeds change. And this very change is fundamental in our progress as a species. But as I have said in my previous works, progress alone is not enough, that progress must be humane, if not, then such progress is of no value. Let's assume that we make great strides in terms of progress, but what are we going to do with it if it doesn't have any sweetness whatsoever! A cold, mechanical progress is no progress.

It's not enough to make only external mechanical advancement, equally important is internal psychological advancement. The problem is that we place all our attention on external mechanical advancement and barely any on internal psychological advancement. The situation is so dire that we often tend to measure the advancement of a nation based on their industrial capacities. Industry is not the mark of progress - compassion, reason and self-reliance are.

But even if I and many after me keep reminding humanity of this simple fact thousands and thousands of times, it'll still take our species many millennia if not more to actually practice it as a natural way of life. But here's another fact, no humane future, not even one as distant as several millennia away, can be produced without the humane actions of the humans living today. The sooner we start, the sooner our progeny will grow out of the infancy that we and our ancestors have been living in so far.

So first, throw your stupid arrogance and pride as far away as possible and start afresh - accept the fact that you know nothing, then start from there - become your own teacher - become your own guide - become your own scientist - question everything, learn from everything and stop at nothing. Keep moving ahead, with your head held high and integrity upright.

A handful of individuals with head held high and integrity upright are all the gods and saviors the world needs. I am no son of God, I am no prophet of God, I am God itself, so are you and so is every single being of conscience and character. I do not care whether there is an almighty lord up there, all I care is that this is our world and if we don't take responsibility for it, then we better pack up our bags and head back home to the jungle.

As I have said in my previous works, I am not an advocate of God, I am an advocate of godliness. And in case the term godliness is too vague, let me put it this way instead. I am not an advocate of God, I am an advocate of humaneness, for humaneness is godliness. Feel humane, think humane, act humane - this is the whole of religion, that is, this is the whole of religion in a civilized and thinking society.

The more primitive a society, the more its religion is infested with bigotry, prejudice, rituals and ceremonies. A civilized religion places its focus on humans first, then everything else, whereas a primitive religion holds rituals, ceremonies and images to be of supreme significance and demands absolute allegiance to these rituals, ceremonies and images from the humans whom it deems sinners.

As I said earlier, everything must evolve, if it doesn't it either gets destroyed or destroys the world. Don't get stuck my friend, for if you get stuck with rigidity, the whole world will get stuck with rigidity and our children will face nothing but prejudice wherever they go.

We have already started to become a global species, so, now more than ever, we must take every step to strengthen and humanize that globalization. We must breathe inclusion into the society with our actions - not should, but must. Rigidity of any kind must be thrown away at once.

10. People over Possession

Assimilation is the lifeblood of a civilized society. Technology, innovation, revenue generation, all later, first assimilation - if there is assimilation in your heart, you'll prosper in whatever you do, but if there is no assimilation in you, all your undertakings are bound to fail sooner or later. In fact, that's exactly the direction in which our materialistic society is heading.

Too much entrepreneurial attitude and too little humane accountability, that's the problem with today's world. And such attitude may make life comfortable for the already privileged class, but it does very little for those who are in actual need of basic life-sustaining resources. We are so obsessed with gathering resources after resources that we have absolutely turned blind to those lives with no resources, not even the most basic ones.

And a life that ignores the miseries of others is no human life. Hunger, poverty - all these are there because of our lack of accountability. Those with most to give are obsessed with gaining more, and even when they do give back, in most cases, it's again to gain another form of personal benefit, called tax benefit.

We all are equally responsible for our society, but we simply cannot instill equality in the world so long as most of the world's resources are possessed by only a few - the billionaires, the entrepreneurs, or whatever. And we cannot eliminate hunger and poverty without humanizing the entrepreneurs.

But the question is, can anybody, say I, "make" those entrepreneurs humane? And the answer is no - I cannot. Entrepreneurs must wake up themselves – they must wake up with the call of accountability - an accountability that compels them to not accept a ridiculous amount of non-essential salary and invest it along with a huge portion of their company's revenue in social welfare projects. The day the world learns to measure the net worth of an entrepreneur based on their direct involvement in social welfare and not with money, is the day we'll begin to make substantial strides in eradicating poverty and hunger.

If a billionaire really starts doing actual humanitarian work in their fullest capacity, they would stop being billionaires. Now I don't pretend to understand the economic complexities of a society built by an infant species such as us, but what should be clear to any being of clear conscience is that economic disparities are not born due to these complexities but due to the lack of accountability. And I take immense pleasure in saying that I have come across certain entrepreneurs who are indeed going against the capitalist norm and taking tangible steps to distribute their wealth equally and efficiently through welfare initiatives among their employees and their communities. Remember, human welfare is human duty.

11. First Duty of Humans

We still have a long way to go - the goal is to build a functional self-correcting societal paradigm (the best paradigm is no paradigm, but humans aren't mature enough to maintain order in the society without some sort of paradigm to guide them, not yet) where no human will suffer from the lack of fundamentals in life. And to make this happen, our first duty is to start working on equal distribution of resources. At the same time, we must take a hard look at our necessities and luxuries.

Let me give you an example. Whenever you have some extra money and you think of buying something fancy, ask yourself, do you really need that product, or are you just trying to fill the holes in your life with more possessions? If your conscience tells you that you don't really need it, then use that money to empower a small local business in some way, or perhaps raise some funds among friends and help someone in your neighborhood to set up a business or use those funds to fix the problems of your neighborhood. Find out where the money is needed most and use it there.

Money is an important resource, quite like fossil fuel. Hence it must not be used haphazardly.

However, while with haphazard use of fossil fuel we'll one day run out of it completely and in the process ruin the climate of our planet to the point of no return, haphazard use of money on the other hand will create more economic disparities in the society, almost to the point of no return. So, use money wisely.

The money you own is not yours to abuse, it's an active part of the global economic vehicle, which means, even a slight abuse on your part will lead the vehicle to malfunction, so use as little as possible based on your actual needs and give the rest back into the society in whichever way you see fit. For example, if you need to buy a cell and you have a thousand dollars for it, then instead of wasting the entire thousand dollars on one phone, use three hundred dollars for it, and with the rest buy some food and clothes from street vendors and distribute them among the homeless people in the block. This way you are not only buying a cellphone, but also empowering small businesses as well as helping the poor. And that's the way to end economic disparities.

Remember, every time you waste money on nonessentials, you are essentially contributing to the economic disparities of the world. The point is, no possession can give you the happiness that you'd receive by seeing the smile on someone's face because of you. Remember, possessions can be replaced, not people.

It's not enough to shout about equality, we must feel it, mean it and act on it. We must practice it in our everyday life. To raise a society with the characteristic of equality in its veins, we must feel equal ourselves, not superior, not inferior, but equal. Once we do genuinely feel equal, that very feeling will make us work to instill that equality in our society - it will compel us with the gentle nudge of accountability to make sure that everybody has access to the fundamentals of living.

You cannot simply waste money on the newest model of the iPhone, when countless homes across the world can't even afford electricity. You cannot simply have food fights in the name of fun, when countless people across the world don't even have two wholesome meals in a day. You cannot simply waste a ridiculous amount of money on fancy suits, dresses, wines, cars and mansions when our very own kind is suffering on a daily basis round the clock.

However, I am not talking about giving money to charity, although it's not a bad alternative when you cannot get involved more directly for whatever reason. I am talking about being a whole human being, which means keeping your necessities at bare minimum and using the rest of your resources in lifting others. The less your needs, the stronger your integrity.

The greatest contribution is the contribution of one's existence. If you cannot do that, do whatever you can, not due to some moral compulsion, but because of an existential responsibility. Give because the act of giving gives you pleasure, not because you like to hear good things about yourself.

12. No One Culture is Enough

If everyone practices giving at their fullest capacity, there wouldn't be any disparity in the world. Act human and watch the disparities disappear in front of your eyes. You cannot change the world overnight, but you can change it one act at a time. Some may say, why should we try to change the world, isn't the smart thing to do is to adapt to the world! To them I say, adapting to inhumanity is not smartness, it's stupidity. So, you decide, are you being smart by accepting things as they are, or quite the opposite!

I do not accept savagery - I do not accept indifference - I do not accept narcissism - I do not accept bigotry - I do not accept discrimination and sectarianism, be it in the name of religion, gender or culture. Remember, it's the people that make a culture, but over time people become secondary and culture becomes all-important, and that's where all the trouble begins.

In an attempt to defend one's own culture, humans start acting like savages, quite similar to our primitive ancestors. Remember, culture may be a part of us, but it must never take over us, for the moment it does, the subconscious notion of "us versus them" begins to fester in the mind, leading to nothing but death and destruction.

That's why I denounced my savage obedience to the culture I was born in in my teenage years, and kept looking for more. One culture was not enough for me, I had to feel all the cultures of the world rushing through my veins filling up every molecule in my body - it was a burning desire - as urgent as the thirst of a person who hasn't had water for months.

Hence, I assimilated as many cultures as possible, made them one with my existence and have presented them in my works, but my assimilation is far from complete - so long as I live this assimilation will continue. Perhaps only then, five hundred years after I am gone, humans from every corner of the world will be able to see themselves in me.

As long as there is even a single community of thinking humans who could say I am not their own, I'll consider my mission to be incomplete. I must belong to everyone, or else my life is worthless, for belonging to the whole of humanity is what makes us human. That's why I keep telling people who approach me during my travels and ask about my writing, that I am no writer, I am only an example of humanity.

In short, I am a living representation of my species - I am not owned by any one culture, but all cultures live through me - I am not owned by any one belief system, but all belief systems are part of me - I am not owned by any one school of thought, but all schools of thought are born in me. However, at the same time I must admit, I have more ignorance than knowledge - I have had more failures than successes - I have had more impediments than aids - but my sight has always been wider than my abilities permit - and that's the reason why I exist as a beacon of universalism on the face of earth.

Here some may wonder, am I talking about myself or my species - to them I say, what's the difference! The difference is a mere delusion. Step outside your conditionings and the difference will disappear. I am my species, my species is me. In me you'll see the species, in the species you'll see me. In me you'll see yourself, in yourself you'll find me. In yourself you'll see the species, in the species you'll find yourself.

Live to assimilate, not to discriminate. Discrimination is the mark of a savage, assimilation is the mark of a sage. But don't take the sage as some sort of superior human, for a sage is anything but superior human - a sage is simply a plain ordinary human being who has understood the value of human life beyond the petty squabbles of societal brandings.

You don't need to go into the jungle and spend years alone in meditation to become a sage, all you got to do, or I should say, all you need to feel, is a sense of belonging with the humans from all over the world. If you feel that, and I mean, if you feel that in the most practical fashion, and in not in some primitive, mystical fashion, then you are a sage. Every sage is a true human, but not every human is a sage. But I say again, here your purpose is not to find a proper label to stick on your forehead, but to find the purpose itself and give all to that purpose. Once you find your purpose, every day lived is a lifetime lived.

13. Antidote to Misery

The question is not how long will you live, the question is, if you die tomorrow, will your name be alive even after a hundred years! Immortality is a byproduct of service. Annihilate yourself for a cause and you'll be remembered for eternity by the people who are worth remembered by.

For example, in schools kids are taught about Edison to be the greatest inventor of all times, but when some of those kids grow up to be actual rational human beings with the capacity for thinking, they denounce the fake glory of Edison (at least as an inventor) and start idolizing Tesla, for if any one person rightfully deserves the title of the greatest inventor of all times, it's Nikola Tesla.

Edison was an entrepreneur, not an inventor. He was like the Steve Jobs of his time, who rarely had any original idea of his own, if any, whereas the mind of Nikola Tesla was the breeding grounds of inventions that has fundamentally shaped our life in 21st century. Today Tesla is gone, but his contribution lives on through every single person who uses electricity and internet.

The point is, your work may or may not bring you recognition in your lifetime, but recognition is not the purpose of your work, if it is, then all your endeavors are in vain. Now, I am not saying that there won't be any expectation, for it is a biological impossibility, rather what I am saying is that, don't feed such occasional expectations.

We are an organic species, as such we will always have occasional waves of expectations, just like we'll always have occasional waves of sorrows and desperation, but we mustn't be driven by them or attached to them, instead let them be and work through them. Work is the antidote to misery.

With work misery is relieved, with laziness misery is multiplied. While there is genuine misery in the world, there is also misery that is born of nothing but laziness, snobbery and selfishness. The former is mostly imposed by circumstances, whereas the latter is simply self-imposed. However, the antidote for both is action. You can sit on your couch crying your brains out, but that won't change your situation, to change the situation you have to step up and act - you have to act through your sorrows.

You have a brain which is literally the smartest and most advanced one on earth, that too among about 8.7 million species. Do you comprehend the gravitas of the matter? It is not something to be taken for granted. What this means is that, if you set your heart to it and act, there is nothing you cannot accomplish, given that you are never ever ready to give up, no matter how many obstructions and failures come your way. Neither fortune, nor opportunity, nor ancestry, nor wealth - nothing determines your destiny - there is only one question that determines your destiny - will you give up after coming all this way?

Give up or not, it's your business, but never blame it on fortune, for fortune is slave to the determined and master to the weakling. Human brain is the supreme creator of all fortune. It is the biggest miracle of nature (in relation to life on earth) which makes all other miracles possible. In short, you are the miracle maker yourself, quite literally speaking. If you are determined and persistent in your endeavors, then the result will appear as nothing short of miracle to others. It has nothing to do with magic and mysticism or divine intervention, it simply has to do with your indomitable will to keep moving forward. If you keep moving ahead, miracle will keep manifesting, but if you stop, miracles will stop.

Remember, a civilization is born of a civilized mind, and one of the fundamental characteristics of a civilized mind is action. Without action no civilization can survive the obstacles of time, no matter how much they wish, pray and hope. Be civilized my friend, not in name only, but in action. Remember, indifference suits roaches, not humans. So, step up and act with all your might, sight and light.

14. Endless Supply of Courage

No matter how strengthless you feel at times, there is always some strength you can foster to pierce through the darkness. Because no strength comes from outside, it is born in you. There is no such thing as a perpetual motion engine, except the human mind (metaphorically speaking), that is, it can never - I repeat, it can never ever run out of courage - yes at times, it may feel like there is no courage left in you, and that's very much human as well, but the moment you remind yourself why you are doing what you are doing, your brain starts producing all the courage you need. You are the vessel of courage as well as the manufacturer.

Courage, compassion, conscience (also creativity) - all these have no end - they are truly limitless - so long as your brain is healthy and functioning, you won't ever run out of courage, compassion and conscience. All power is born of your nerves, literally speaking. So if you run out of courage, the world will run out of courage - if you run out of conscience, the world will run out of conscience - if you run out of compassion, the world will run out of compassion.

Fortunately for us, as I said earlier, a healthy human brain never runs out of courage, conscience and compassion. So, be what you want to be - do what you want to do - for there is no power in any obstacle that can overcome the power of a determined brain, that is, a determined mind.

But again, doing what you want is not a big deal, even an animal can do that, what is human is to do what is best for not just the self but the society as well. Courage that benefits only you is nothing but animal courage, it's only human courage when it benefits others. Courage is merely a tool, how you use it, determines what you are. Use your courage to defend the weak - use your courage to help the helpless - use your courage to fortify the destitute - only then will your courage be deemed human - only then will you be deemed human - not by me, not by you, but by time.

Bring out all your limitless torrents of courage and offer your life at the feet of the people and your sacrifice will turn the breath of even the most innocent commoner into a purifying movement. Your courage will be a reminder for people of their own courage. Stand tall as an unbending flag of courage with your feet firmly and humbly placed on the soil of society and all the people will stand by you as soldiers in the making of an actual civilized planet.

15. Thoughts over Instincts

Civilization starts with you, but it won't so long as you keep letting your instincts drive you through your life. Thoughts - civilized and conscientious thoughts - that's what'll take you and the world forward, whereas instincts will only take you backward (not all though, for some instincts will keep playing an intricate role in the human society, say, a newborn's instinct to grab on to the breast one its own to sustain itself).

Instincts are older, but thoughts are recent, that's why instincts are more powerful than thoughts - that's why it takes great will power to express a thought through action, while instincts come so easily. However, if we continue practicing our thoughts long enough, eventually the instincts that hold power over us will turn powerless. And this my friend, ought to be the next step of our evolution, and that's why it's no longer merely a matter of natural selection, it's what I hereby dub "sapient selection", that is the process of determining the path of our evolution ourselves.

The instincts won't go away for a long time from our neuroanatomy as I have said many times in my previous works, but you are no longer at their mercy any more, unlike our fellow animal species. We have developed the capacity of awareness beyond the wildest dreams of any animal species. All living organism has awareness, for awareness is the fundamental ingredient of life, without which life cannot exist, but we humans are at the very top of the ladder of awareness, in terms of complexity, whereas all other species are way down below.

You see, the wilderness is run by instincts, that's why it remains wilderness, but when a species starts to gain control of its instincts, it no longer is at the mercy of the wild and it would eventually be able to build a civilized society. So far, only we the humans have started to walk in that direction - I say, we have only started, because we still have a long way to go till we are completely free from the internal oppression of our instincts.

It's these instincts that make inhumanities like racism, misogyny, phobia, fundamentalism and bigotry prevail. So, the very fact that they exist indicates that we have not yet succeeded in overpowering our instincts. We have the capacity to do so, yes, but it doesn't mean we use it. And this is the reason why though we look human, doesn't mean we act human. The day we get hold of our instincts is the day we become truly human.

16. When Strength Calls

Human is not a species - human is a promise - a promise to never stop growing - a promise to never stop learning from our mistakes - a promise to acknowledge our shortcomings and sharpen our strengths. The biggest mistake is to make no mistake. Mistakes bring understanding - we learn more by being wrong than by being right. Only by recognizing our mistakes, our shortcomings, can we be sure of our strengths.

Do you know what strength is - forgetting sleep, romance, money I keep working without rest to unite the humans, that's my strength - a single mother working day and night so her child can have a bright future, that's her strength - a street vendor working hard since dawn for his family, that's his strength. Do you have such a strength of your own? Your ancestry, your family money, your material possessions - putting aside all these, what is your own true strength?

Find out that strength and give your fullest lifeforce to that strength, and you will witness the dawn of a new, rejuvenated, headstrong civilization. There is nothing wrong in being headstrong, in fact, to dream the impossible dream, to reach the unreachable goal, to cross the uncrossable sea, you have to be headstrong, but make sure you are headstrong for the right reasons, because while being headstrong the moment you give in to impulses, is the moment when there is no longer any difference between you and a ferocious animal of the wild.

You are strong - strongest among all the living species on earth - don't let anybody tell you otherwise - don't give in to the discouraging ramblings of the so-called practical people. Accepting weakness as the usual state of life is not practicality, it's foolishness at its worst. Weakness is a natural part of life, yes, but it's not the usual state of life - it's not the whole of life. For the shallow, weakness is discouraging, but for the wise, weakness is opportunity to take inventory of one's strength.

Recognize your strength and work through your weakness. Life is too precious and brief to be wasted on entertaining weakness. Life is grand, so should be the way of living. But mark you, by grand I am not talking about sophisticated living, by grand I am referring to living at our fullest. To live beyond fears - to live beyond weakness - to live beyond insecurity - that's what living grand is all about. Remember, beyond fear there is clarity - beyond weakness there is victory - beyond insecurity there is life.

17. Wake Up from Death

Wake up from death my friend and return to life. You have been dead for long, since the moment you were born, now it's time to wake up - a lot is to be done - a lot is to be achieved - a lot is to be discovered. Life is for discovery, not sleep. So, sleep not any more and leap to the realization of your purpose. And whatever your purpose is, make sure it benefits the society in some way. Because if your purpose serves only you and nobody else, then it's no purpose of a civilized human, but merely a waste of life. Life is only life when its interests are intertwined with the benefits of others. And here, there is no place for any sectarianism whatsoever - not religion, not gender, not sexuality, nothing.

Take a glass of water, now tell me, is it Christian water, or Jewish water, or Islamic water or Atheist water. It's just water. A human ought to be like that water, whose purpose is to quench the thirst of humans, not of any specific religion, culture or gender, but all humans. Humans without borders, that's what the world needs - beings of conscience and courage, with no rigidity of religion, gender, nationality, or any other.

Rigidity and civilization can never go together. As long as there is even a trace of rigidity, you are not living with your full potential. Rigidity is bondage that keeps you from realizing your true capacity. Once you renounce all your rigidity, every molecule in your body will be saturated with potential - your mind will travel so fast and wide, that your body will fall short in front of the vastness of your mind.

Sometimes my mind travels so far ahead that my body can barely keep up, that's the reason why I never run out of ideas. I am exploding with so many ideas every day that I am barely able to put them down on paper. If I could write every single idea that appears in my head, an entire library will fall short for my books.

In the beginning, it was me who controlled the words, but soon the words acquired full control of my mind, and now my mind acts however my words steer it. And since I already had prepared the soil of my mind with the ingredients of love and acceptance, now every idea that is born in it, works in that direction, that is, the direction of universal assimilation.

But mark you, there is nothing magical in this process, yet I know that some people won't be able to help themselves from turning it into yet another mystical story, so let me eliminate all possibilities of mystical nonsense right away. It's as simple as this. If you can devote your existence to one purpose, to such an extent that you breathe that purpose, dream that purpose and live that purpose, then your mind automatically gets rewired as per your will to serve that purpose.

What this means is that your mind will never stop working on that purpose, and I mean never, that is, even when you are not consciously thinking of that purpose. Your mind will work on your purpose when you are sleeping - your mind will work on your purpose when you are doing your daily chores - basically your mind, that is, your brain, will allot a huge portion of its energy to consistently work on that purpose, regardless of time and place.

To put it simply, once you willingly devote yourself to a purpose, that purpose of your life no longer remains just the conscious focus of your mind, more importantly it becomes the subconscious focus. And this capacity is no exclusive possession of a handful of so-called geniuses, rather it's a universal capacity. All you need to do is recognize your own unique purpose and give everything you have to that purpose and you will do wonders, for you own the most magnificent wonder of nature, the human brain.

18. Valor in Civilized Society

There is power in you to either make the world or break the world - so what will it be? Will you keep on fostering baseless primitive hate and prejudice against people on the savage grounds of nation, race, religion, sexuality and so on, or will you actually start practicing your humanhood?

To slaughter people, either in mind or in action, in the name of tribe is valor of the stone age, to love a stranger as our own family is valor of a civilized society. To empower them, to defend them, to die for them, that's the valor of a civilized society - it's the very definition of humanhood. Do you have that valor my friend - do you have such humanhood in your marrows? Remember, either we'll stand together or we'll get extinct.

Power doesn't mean to control people, real power is to bring happiness in their lives. Unless you practice that power, you are good as dead. What is death - death is not when your body stops working, death is when your humanity stays asleep. Till you wake up your humanity, life is but a vessel of death.

Awake, arise, be the vessel of life and humanity, not of death and savagery. Too many people are living like that, as vessels of death and savagery, but not you, for you are responsible, you are accountable - you are accountable for what happens to your neighborhood, you are accountable for what happens to our society, you are accountable for what happens to our world. And a person with accountability can never sit still and watch the world burn to ashes due to primitive stupidity. So, you must rise, you must rise with a heart of honey and nerves of steel.

Rise so that even the weakest feels invigorated. The only way to instill courage in the society is to be the courage incarnate ourselves - the only way to instill conscience in the society is to be the conscience incarnate ourselves - the only way to instill compassion in the society is to be the compassion incarnate ourselves. It all starts with us - it all starts with you.

If you are accountable, the world will be accountable - if you are irresponsible, the world is bound to be irresponsible. Accountability is the magic potion of order, not law, not government, not industry, but the accountability in each of us. So step up and be accountable - step up and be a hero - step up and be a human.

BIBLIOGRAPHY

Aristotle. Politics. Penguin; Revised, Reprint edition. (2000)

Aristotle. De Anima (On the Soul). Penguin Random House. 1987

Aristotle. Physics. Kessinger Publishing, 2004

Archer M., (2000), Being Human: The Problem of Agency. Cambridge University Press.

Archer M., (2003), Structure, Agency and the Internal Conversation. Cambridge University Press.

Adolphs R (2003) Cognitive neuroscience of human social behaviour. Nature Rev Neurosci 4: 165–178.

Adolphs R, Tranel D, Damasio AR (2003) Dissociable neural systems for recognizing emotions. Brain Cogn 52: 61–69.

Afton, A. D. (1985). Forced copulation as a reproductive strategy of male lesser scaup: A field test of some predictions. - Behaviour 92, p. 146-167.

Allison T, Puce A, McCarthy G. (2000) Social perception from visual cues: role of the STS region. Trends Cogn Sci 4: 267–278.

Andresen, Jensine, and Robert Forman, eds. Cognitive Models and Spiritual Maps. Bowling Green, Ohio: Imprint Academic, 2000.

Ashbrook, James, and Carol Albright. The Humanizing Brain: Where Religion and Neuroscience Meet. Cleveland, OH: Pilgrim Press, 1997.

Azari, Nina, Janpeter Nickel, Gilbert Wunderlich, Michael Niedeggen, Harald Hefter, Lutz Tellmann, Hans Herzog, Petra Stoerig, Dieter Birnbacher, and Rudiger Seitz. "Neural Correlates of Religious Experience."

European Journal of Neuroscience 13, no. 8 (2001)

Agar, N. (2004). Liberal eugenics: In defence of human enhancement. London: Blackwell Publishing.

Alteheld, N., Roessler, G., Vobig, M., & Walter, R. (2004). The retina implant new approach to a visual prosthesis. Biomedizinische Technik, 49(4), 99–103.

Antal, A., Nitsche, M. A., Kincses, T. Z., Kruse, W., Hoffmann, K. P., & Paulus, W. (2004a). Facilitation of visuo-motor learning by transcranial direct current stimulation of the motor and extrastriate visual areas in humans. European Journal of Neuroscience, 19(10), 2888–2892.

Bhat Z, Kumar, S, Bhat H (2015) In vitro meat production. Challenges and benefits over conventional meat production. J Sci Food Agric 14: 241–248

Bernstein R. J., (1967), John Dewey. New York: Washington Square Press.

Bernstein R.J., (1971), Praxis and Action: Contemporary Philosophies of Human Activity. Philadelphia: University of Pennsylvania Press.

Bernstein R.J., (1976), The Restructuring Social and Political Thought.

Bernstein R.J., (1983), Beyond Relativism and Objectivism: Science, Hermeneutics, and Praxis. Philadelphia: University of Pennsylvania Press.

Bernstein R.J., (1986), Philosophical Profiles. Philadelphia: University of Pennsylvania Press.

Bernstein R.J., (1991), New Constellation. Cambridge: MIT Press.

Barash, D. P. (1977). Sociobiology of rape in mallards (Anas platyrhynchos):

Responses of the mated male. - Science 197, p. 788-789.

Berger, J. (1986). Wild horses of the great basin: Social competition and population size. - The University of Chicago Press, Chicago.

Birkhead, T. R., Johnson, S. D. & Nettleship, D. N. (1985). Extra-pair matings and mate guarding in the common murre Uria aalge. - Anim. Behav. 33, p. 608-619.

Beauregard, Mario, and Vincent Paquette. "Neural Correlates of a Mystical Experience in Carmelite Nuns." Neuroscience Letters 405, no. 3 (2006)

Benson, Herbert. Timeless Healing: The Power and Biology of Belief. New York: Scribner, 1996

Bogen, J.E.(1995a), 'On the neurophysiology of consciousness: Part I. An overview', Consciousness and Cognition, 4.

Bogen, J.E. (1995b), 'On the neurophysiology of consciousness: Part II. Constraining the semantic problem', Consciousness and Cognition, 4.

Bremner, J. D., R. Soufer, et al. (2001). "Gender differences in cognitive and neural correlates of remembrance of emotional words." Psychopharmacol Bull 35 (3).

Brothers, L. (2002). The social brain: A project for integrating primate behavior and neurophysiology in a new domain. In J. T. Cacioppo et al. (Eds.), Foundations in neuroscience. Cambridge, MA: MIT Press.

Buss, D. D. (2003). Evolutionary Psychology: The New Science of Mind, 2nd ed. New York: Allyn & Bacon.

Buss, D. M. (1989). "Conflict between the sexes: Strategic interference and the evocation of anger and upset." J Pers Soc Psychol 56 (5).

Buss, D. M. (1995). "Psychological sex differences. Origins through sexual selection." Am Psychol 50 (3).

Buss, D. M. (2002). "Review: Human Mate Guarding." Neuro Endocrinol Lett 23 (Suppl 4).

Buss, D. M., and D. P. Schmitt (1993). "Sexual strategies theory: An evolutionary perspective on human mating." Psychol Rev 100 (2).

Blakemore SJ, Decety J (2001) From the perception of action to the understanding of intention. Nature Rev Neurosci 2: 561.

Bruce C, Desimone R, Gross CG (1981) Visual properties of neurons in a polysensory area in superior temporal sulcus of the macaque. J Neurophysiol 46: 369–384.

Buccino G, Vogt S, Ritzl A, Fink GR, Zilles K, Freund HJ, Rizzolatti G (2004) Neural circuits underlying imitation of hand actions: an event related fMRI study. Neuron 42: 323–34.

Colapietro V., (1988), "Human Agency: The Habits of Our Being." Southern Journal of Philosophy, XXVI, 2, pp. 153-68.

Colapietro V., (1992), "Purpose, Power, and Agency." The Monist, 75, 4 (October) pp. 423-44.

Colapietro V., (2003), "Signs and their vicissitudes: Meanings in excess of consciousness and functionality." Logica, Dialogica, Ideologica, a cure di Susan Petrilli e Patrizia Calefato (Milano: Mimesis), pp. 221-36.

Colapietro V., (2004a), "C. S. Peirce's Reclamation of Teleology." Nature in American Philosophy, ed. Jean De Groot (Washington, D.C.: Catholic University Press of America), pp. 88-108.

Colapietro V., (2004b), "Portrait of a Historicist: An Alternative Reading of

Peircean Semiotic." Semiotiche, 2/04 [maggio 2004], pp. 49-68.

Colapietro V., (2006), "Engaged Pluralism: Between Alterity and Sociality." The Pragmatic Century: Conversations with Richard J. Bernstein (Albany, NY: SUNY Press), pp. 39-68.

Colapietro V., (2009), "Habit, Competence, and Purpose." Forthcoming in The Transactions of the Charles S. Peirce Society. Calder AJ, Keane J, Manes F, Antoun N, Young AW (2000) Impaired recognition and experience of disgust following brain injury. Nature Neurosci 3: 1077–1078.

Carey DP, Perrett DI, Oram MW (1997) Recognizing, understanding and reproducing actions. In: Jeannerod M, Grafman J (eds) Handbook of neuropsychology. Vol. 11: Action and cognition. Elsevier, Amsterdam.

Carr L, Iacoboni M, Dubeau MC, Mazziotta JC, Lenzi GL (2003) Neural mechanisms of empathy in humans: a relay from neural systems for imitation to limbic areas. Proc Natl Acad Sci USA 100: 5497–5502.

Changeux JP, Ricoeur P (1998) La nature et la règle. Odile Jacob, Paris.

Cochin S, Barthelemy C, Roux S, Martineau J (1999) Observation and execution of movement: similarities demonstrated by quantified electroencephalograpy. Eur J Neurosci 11: 1839– 1842.

Chomsky Noam, (2017) Requiem for the American Dream

Chomsky Noam, (2016) Who Rules the World?

Chomsky Noam, (2010) How the World Works

Churchland, P.S. (1986), Neurophilosophy (Cambridge, MA: The MIT Press).

Churchland, P.S. & Ramachandran, V.S. (1993), 'Filling in: Why Dennett is wrong', in Dennett and His Critics: Demystifying Mind, ed. B. Dahlbom (Oxford: Blackwell Scientific Press).

Churchland, P.S., Ramachandran, V.S. & Sejnowski, T.J. (1994), 'A critique of pure vision', in Large- scale Neuronal Theories of the Brain, ed. C. Koch & J.L. Davis (Cambridge, MA: The MIT Press).

Crick, F. (1994), The Astonishing Hypothesis: The Scientific Search for the Soul (New York: Simon and Schuster).

Crick, F. (1996), 'Visual perception: rivalry and consciousness', Nature, 379.

Crick, F. & Koch, C. (1992), 'The problem of consciousness', Scientific American, 267.

Craig AD (2002) How do you feel? Interoception: the sense of the physiological condition of the body. Nature Rev Neurosci 3: 655–666.

Damasio, A (2003a) Looking for Spinoza. Harcourt Inc. Damasio A (2003b) Feeling of emotion and the self. Ann NY Acad Sci 1001: 253–261.

d'Aquili, Eugene. "Senses of Reality in Science and Religion." Zygon 17, no 4 (1982)

d'Aquili, Eugene. "The Biopsychological Determinants of Religious Ritual Behavior." Zygon 10, no. 1 (1975)

d'Aquili, Eugene. "The Myth-Ritual Complex: A Biogenetic Structural Analysis." Zygon 18, no. 3 (1983) d'Aquili, Eugene, and Andrew Newberg. The Mystical Mind: Probing the Biology of Religious Experience. Minneapolis: Fortress Press, 1999.

Daly DD. 1958. Ictal affect. Am J Psychiatry.

Damasio, A. (1994) Descartes' Error: Emotion, Reason and the Human Brain. New York, Putnams.

Damasio, A. (1999) The Feeling of What Happens: Body, Emotion and the Making of Consciousness. London, Heinemann.

Darwin, C. (1859) On the Origin of Species by Means of Natural Selection. London, Murray.

Darwin, C. (1871) The Descent of Man and Selection in Relation to Sex. London, John Murray.

Darwin, C. (1872) The Expression of the Emotions in Man and Animals. London, John Murray; also published

1965, Chicago, University of Chicago Press.

Dawkins, M.S. (1987) Minding and mattering. In C. Blakemore and S. Greenfield (eds) Mindwaves. Oxford, Blackwell, 151-60.

Dawkins, R. (1976) The Selfish Gene. Oxford, Oxford University Press; a new edition, with additional material, was published in 1989.

Dawkins, R. (1986) The Blind Watchmaker. London, Longman.

Di Pellegrino G, Fadiga L, Fogassi L, Gallese V, Rizzolatti G (1992) Understanding motor events: A neurophysiological study. Exp Brain Res 91: 176–80.

Deikman, A.J. (2000) A functional approach to mysticism. Journal of Consciousness Studies 7(11-12), 75-91.

Delmonte, M.M. (1987) Personality and meditation. In M. West (ed.) The

Psychology of Meditation. Oxford, Clarendon Press, 118-32.

Dennett, D.C. (1987) The Intentional Stance. Cambridge, MA, MIT Press.

Dennett, D.C. (1988) Quining qualia. In A.J. Marcel and E. Bisiach (eds) Consciousness in Contemporary Science. Oxford, Oxford University Press, 42-77.

Dennett, D.C. (1991) Consciousness Explained. Boston, MA, and London, Little, Brown and Co.

Dennett, D.C. (1995a) Darwin's Dangerous Idea. London, Penguin.

Dennett, D.C. (1995b) The unimagined preposterousness of zombies. Journal of Consciousness Studies 2(4), 322-6.

Dennett, D.C. (1995c) Cog: steps towards consciousness in robots. In T. Metzinger (ed.) Conscious Experience. Thorverton, Devon, Imprint Academic, 471-87.

Dennett, D.C. (1995d) The path not taken. Behavioral and Brain Sciences 18, 252-3; commentary on N. Block, On a confusion about a function of consciousness. Behavioral and Brain Sciences 18, 227.

Dennett, D.C. (1996a) Facing backwards on the problem of consciousness. Journal of Consciousness Studies 3(1), 4-6.

Dennett, D.C. (1996b) Kinds of Minds: Towards an Understanding of Consciousness. London, Weidenfeld & Nicolson.

Dennett, D.C. (1997) An exchange with Daniel Dennett. In J. Searle (ed.) The Mystery of Consciousness. New York, New York Review of Books, 115-19.

Dennett, D.C. (1998) The myth of double transduction. In S.R. Hameroff, A.W. Kaszniak and A. C. Scott (eds) Toward a Science of Consciousness: The Second Tucson Discussions and

Debates. Cambridge, MA, MIT Press, 97-107.

Dennett, D.C. (1998b) Brainchildren: Essays on Designing Minds. Cambridge, MA, MIT Press.

Dennett, D.C. (2001) The fantasy of first person science. Debate with D. Chalmers, Northwestern University, Evanston, IL, February 2001.

Dennett, D.C. (2003) Freedom Evolves. New York, Penguin.

Dennett, D.C. and Kinsbourne, M. (1992) Time and the observer: the where and when of consciousness in the brain. Behavioral and Brain Sciences 15, 183-247, including commentaries and authors' responses.

Dewey J., (1911 [1977]), "Epistemological Realism: The Alleged Ubiquity of the Knowledge Relation." Journal of Philosophy, VIII, 20 (September 28, 1911).

Dewhurst, Kenneth, and A. W. Beard. "Sudden Religious Conversions in Temporal Lobe Epilepsy." British Journal of Psychiatry 117 (1970)

Dewhurst K, Beard AW. Sudden religious conversions in temporal lobe epilepsy. 1970 Epilepsy Behav 2003

Devinsky O, Lai G. Spirituality and religion in epilepsy. Epilepsy Behav 2008.

Devinsky, O., Morrell, MJ, Vogt, BA. (1995) 'Contribution of anterior cingulate cortex to behavior', Brain, 118.

Douglas Stone A., Chapter 24, The Indian Comet, in the book Einstein and the Quantum, Princeton University Press, Princeton, New Jersey, 2013.

E. Horvitz, "One Hundred Year Study on Artificial Intelligence: Reflections and Framing," ed: Stanford University, 2014.

Einstein A. (1925). "Quantentheorie des einatomigen idealen Gases". Sitzungsberichte der Preussischen Akademie der Wissenschaften.

Eckhart Meister, Selected Writings

Egidi R., ed. (1999), "Von Wright and 'Dante's Dream': Stages in a Philosophical Pilgrim's Progress", in In Search of a New Humanism: the Philosophy of G.H. von Wright, ed. by R. Egidi, Kluwer, Dordrecht.

Fadiga L, Fogassi L, Pavesi G, Rizzolatti G (1995) Motor facilitation during action observation: a magnetic stimulation study. J Neurophysiol 73: 2608–2611.

Fogassi L, Gallese V, Fadiga L, Rizzolatti G (1998) Neurons responding to the sight of goal directed hand/arm actions in the parietal area PF (7b) of the macaque monkey. Soc Neurosci Abs 24:257.5.

Frith U, Frith CD (2003) Development and neurophysiology of mentalizing. Philos Trans R Soc Lond B Biol Sci 358: 459.

Farah, M.J. (1989), 'The neural basis of mental imagery', Trends in Neurosciences, 10.

Finlay BL, Darlington RB (1995) Linked regularities in the development and evolution of mammalian brains. Science 268.

Freud, S. "The Interpretation of Dreams", 1900

Freud, S. "Selected papers on hysteria and other psychoneuroses" Journal of Nervous and Mental Disease 1909.

Freud, S. "The Origin and Development of Psychoanalysis", 1910

Freud, S. "Psychopathology of everyday life", 1914

Freud, S. "Beyond the Pleasure Principle", 1920

Frith, C.D. & Dolan, R.J. (1997), 'Abnormal beliefs: Delusions and memory', Paper presented at the May, 1997, Harvard Conference on Memory and Belief.

Gay, Volney, ed. Neuroscience and Religion. Plymouth, UK: Lexington Books, 2009.

Gazzaniga, M. S. (1985). The social brain. New York: Basic Books.

Gazzaniga, M.S. (1993), 'Brain mechanisms and conscious experience', Ciba Foundation Symposium, 174.

Geschwind N. "Behavioural changes in temporal lobe epilepsy". Psychol Med. 1979.

Gellhorn, E., Kiely, W.F. "Mystical states of consciousness: neurophysiological and clinical aspects." J Nerv Ment Dis. 1972;154:399-405.

Gilbert SL, Dobyns WB, Lahn BT (2005) Genetic links between brain development and brain evolution. Nat Rev Genet 6.

Gray JA. The Psychology of Fear and Stress. 2nd ed. New York, NY: Cambridge University Press; 1988.

Gloor, P. (1992), 'Amygdala and temporal lobe epilepsy', in The Amygdala: Neurobiological Aspects of Emotion, Memory and Mental Dysfunction, ed J.P. Aggleton (New York: Wiley-Liss).

Greenspan, S. I. and S. G. Shanker (2004). The first idea: How symbols, language, and intelligence evolved from our early primate ancestors to modern humans. Cambridge, MA: Da Capo Press.

Grady, D. (1993), 'The vision thing: Mainly in the brain', Discover, June.

Gallagher HL, Frith CD (2003) Functional imaging of 'theory of mind'. Trends Cogn Sci 7: 77.

Gallese V, Fogassi L, Fadiga L, Rizzolatti G (2002) Action representation and the inferior parietal lobule. In: Prinz W, Hommel B (eds) Attention & Performance XIX. Common mechanisms in perception and action. Oxford University Press, Oxford.

Gallese V, Keysers C, Rizzolatti G (2004) A unifying view of the basis of social cognition. Trends Cogn Sci 8: 396–403.

Gangitano M, Mottaghy FM, Pascual-Leone A (2001) Phase specific modulation of cortical motor output during movement observation. NeuroReport 12: 1489–1492.

Gangitano M, Mottaghy FM, Pascual-Leone A (2004) Modulation of premotor mirror neuron activity during observation of unpredictable grasping movements. Eur J Neurosci 20: 2193– 2202.

Goldman AI, Sripada CS (2004) Simulationist models of face-based emotion recognition. Cognition 94: 193–213.

Grèzes J, Costes N, Decety J (1998) Top-down effect of strategy on the perception of human biological motion: a PET investigation. Cogn Neuropsychol 15: 553–582.

Grèzes J, Armony JL, Rowe J, Passingham RE (2003) Activations related to "mirror" and "canonical" neurones in the human brain: an fMRI study. Neuroimage 18: 928–937.

Gross CG, Rocha-Miranda CE, Bender DB (1972) Visual properties of neurons in the inferotemporal cortex of the macaque. J Neurophysiol 35: 96–111.

Hari R, Forss N, Avikainen S, Kirveskari S, Salenius S, Rizzolatti G

(1998) Activation of human primary motor cortex during action observation: a neuromagnetic study. Proc. Natl Acad Sci USA 95: 15061–15065.

Hardy, G. H. (1940). Ramanujan. Cambridge: Cambridge University Press.

Hall, Daniel, Keith Meador, and Harold Koenig. "Measuring Religiousness in Health Research: Review and Critique." Journal of Religion and Health 47, no. 2 (2008)

Harris, Sam, Jonas Kaplan, Ashley Curiel, Susan Bookheimer, Marco Iacoboni, and Mark Cohen. "The Neural Correlates of Religious and Nonreligious Belief." PLoS One 4, no. 10 (October 1, 2009)

Halgren, E. (1992), 'Emotional neurophysiology of the amygdala within the context of human cognition', in The Amygdala:

Neurobiological Aspects of Emotion, Memory and Mental Dysfunction, ed J.P. Aggleton (New York: Wiley-Liss).

Halligan PW, Fink GR, Marshal JC, Vallar G. 2003. Spatial cognition: evidence from visual neglect. Trends Cogn Sci.

Handbook of Emotions, Edited by Michael Lewis, Jeannette M. Haviland-Jones, and Lisa Feldman Barrett, The Guilford Press; 3rd edition (2010).

Haggard, P., Clark, S. and Kalogeras,]. (2002) Voluntary action and conscious awareness, Nature Neuroscience 5, 382-5. Haggard, P., Newman, C. and Magno, E. (1999) On the perceived time of voluntary actions. British Journal of Psychology 90, 291-303.

Hameroff, S.R. and Penrose, R. (1996) Conscious events as orchestrated space-time selections. Journal of Consciousness Studies 3(1), 36-53; also reprinted in J. Shear (ed.) (1997)

Explaining Consciousness-The Hard Problem. Cambridge, MA, MIT Press, 177-95.

Hardcastle, V.G. (2000) How to understand theN in NCC. InT. Metzinger (ed.) Neural Correlates of Consciousness. Cambridge, MA, MIT Press, 259-64.

Harding, D.E. (1961) On Having no Head: Zen and the Re-Discovery of the Obvious. London, Buddhist Society.

Hardy, A. (1979) The Spiritual Nature of Man: A Study of Contemporary Religious Experience. Oxford, Clarendon Press.

Hamad, S. (1990) The symbol grounding problem. Physica D 42, 335-46.

Hamad, S. (2001) No easy way out. The Sciences 41(2), 36-42.

Harre, R. and Gillett, G. (1994) The Discursive Mind. Thousand Oaks, CA, Sage.

Haugeland, J. (ed.) (1997) Mind Design II: Philosophy, Psychology, Artificial Intelligence. Cambridge, MA, MIT Press.

Hauser, M.D. (2000) Wild Minds: What Animals Really Think. New York, Henry Holt and Co.; London, Penguin.

Hearne, K. (1990) The Dream Machine. Northants, Aquarian.

Hebb, D.O. (1949) The Organization of Behavior. New York, Wiley.

Helmholtz, H.L.F. von (1856-67) Treatise on Physiological Optics.

Hess, EH (1975) "The role of pupil size in communication," Scientific American, 233(5), 110–12.

Heyes, C.M. (1998) Theory of mind in nonhuman primates. Behavioral and

Brain Sciences 21, 101-48; with commentaries.

Heyes, C.M. and Galef, B.G. (eds) (1996) Social Learning in Animals: The Roots of Culture. San Diego, CA, Academic Press.

Hilgard, E.R. (1986) Divided Consciousness: Multiple Controls in Human Thought and Action. New York, Wiley.

Hocquette JF (2016) Is in vitro meat the

solution for the future? Meat Science 120:

167–176

Hodgson, R. (1891) A case of double consciousness. Proceedings of the Society for Psychical Research 7, 221-58.

Hofstadter, D.R. (1979) Code!, Escher, Bach: An Eternal Golden Braid. London, Penguin.

Hofstadter, D.R. and Dennett, D.C. (eds) (1981) The Mind's I: Fantasies and Reflections on Self and Soul. London, Penguin.

Holland, J. (ed.) (2001) Ecstasy: The Complete Guide: A Comprehensive Look at the Risks and Benefits of MDMA. Rochester, VT, Park Street Press.

Holmes, D.S. (1987) The influence of meditation versus rest on physiological arousal. In M. West (ed.) The Psychology of Meditation. Oxford, Clarendon Press, 81-103.

Holt, J. (1999) Blindsight in debates about qualia. Journal of Consciousness Studies 6(5), 54-71.

Horgan, J. (1994), 'Can science explain consciousness?', Scientific American, 271.

Holloway RL (1996) Evolution of the human brain. In: Lock A, Peters CR (eds) Handbook of human symbolic evolution. Oxford University Press, Oxford

Iacoboni M, Woods RP, Brass M, Bekkering H, Mazziotta JC, Rizzolatti G (1999) Cortical mechanisms of human imitation. Science 286: 2526–2528.

Iacoboni M, Koski LM, Brass M, Bekkering H, Woods RP, Dubeau MC, Mazziotta JC, Rizzolatti G (2001) Reafferent copies of imitated actions in the right superior temporal cortex. Proc Natl Acad Sci USA 98: 13995–13999.

Jeannerod M (1988) The neural and behavioural organization of goal-directed movements. Clarendon Press, Oxford.

Johnson-Frey SH, Maloof FR, Newman-Norlund R, Farrer C, Inati S, Grafton ST (2003) Actions or hand-objects interactions? Human inferior frontal cortex and action observation. Neuron 39: 1053–1058.

Jackson, F. (1982) Epiphenomenal qualia. Philosophical Quarterly 32, 127-36.

James, W. (1890) The Principles of Psychology (2 volumes). London, Macmillan.

James, W. (1902) The Varieties of Religious Experience: A Study in Human Nature. New York and London, Longmans, Green and Co.

Jansen, K. (2001) Ketamine: Dreams and Realities. Sarasota, FL, Multidisciplinary Association for Psychedelic Studies.

Jay, M. (ed.) (1999) Artificial Paradises: A Drugs Reader. London, Penguin.

Jaynes, J. (1976) The Origin of Consciousness in the Breakdown of the Bicameral Mind. New York, Houghton Mifflin.

Johnson, M.K. and Raye, C.L. (1981) Reality monitoring. Psychological Review 88, 67-85.

Kadim I, Mahgoub O, Baqir S et al. (2015) Cultured meat from muscle stem cells: a review of challenges and prospects. J Integr Agr 14: 222–233

Koski L, Iacoboni M, Dubeau MC, Woods RP, Mazziotta JC (2003) Modulation of cortical activity during different imitative behaviors. J Neurophysiol 89: 460–471.

Krolak-Salmon P, Henaff MA, Isnard J, Tallon-Baudry C, Guenot M, Vighetto A, Bertrand O, Mauguiere F (2003) An attention modulated response to disgust in human ventral anterior insula. Ann Neurol 53: 446–453.

Kandel, E. R. In Search of Memory: The Emergence of a New Science of Mind, W. W. Norton & Company (2007).

Kandel E. R. Schwartz JH, Jessel TM. Principles of neural sciences. New York; McGraw Hill, 2000.

Kanizsa, G. (1979), Organization In Vision (New York: Praeger).

Kaloupek DG, Scott JR, Khatami V. Assessment of coping strategies associated with syncope in blood donors. J Psychosom Res. 1985;29:207-214.

Kanwisher, N. (2001) Neural events and perceptual awareness. Cognition 79, 89-113; also reprinted inS. Dehaene (ed.) The Cognitive Neuroscience of Consciousness. Cambridge, MA, MIT Press, 89-113.

Kapleau, Roshi P. (1980) The Three Pillars of Zen: Teaching, Practice, and Enlightenment (revised edn). New York, Doubleday.

Karn, K. and Hayhoe, M. (2000) Memory representations guide

targeting eye movements in a natural task. Visual Cognition 7, 673-703.

Kasamatsu, A. and Hirai, T. (1966) An electroencephalographic study on the Zen meditation (zazen). Folia Psychiatrica et Neurologica Japonica 20, 315-36.

Kaiserman-Abramof, I. R., Graybiel, A. M., & Nauta, W. J. (1980). The thalamic projection to cortical area 17 in a congenitally anophthalmic mouse strain. Neuroscience, 5, 41–52.

Kanold, P. O., Kara, P., Reid, R. C., & Shatz, C. J. (2003). Role of subplate neurons in functional maturation of visual cortical columns. Science, 301, 521–525.

Kennedy, H., & Dehay, C. (1988). Functional implications of the anatomical organization of the callosal projections of visual areas V1 and V2 in the macaque monkey. Behav. Brain Res., 29, 225–236.

Kentridge, R.W. and Heywood, C.A. (1999) The status of blindsight. Journal of Consciousness Studies 6(5), 3-11.

Kihlstrom, J.F. (1996) Perception without awareness of what is perceived, learning without awareness of what is learned. In M. Velmans (ed.) The Science of Consciousness. London, Routledge, 23-46.

Kollerstrom, N. (1999) The path of Halley's comet, and Newton's late apprehension of the law of gravity. Annals of Science 56, 331-56.

Kosslyn, S.M. (1980) Image and Mind. Cambridge, MA, Harvard University Press.

Kosslyn, S.M. (1988) Aspects of a cognitive neuroscience of mental imagery. Science 240, 1621-6.

Kinsbourne, M. (1995), 'The intralaminar thalamic nucleii', Consciousness and Cognition, 4.

Kjaer, Troels, Camilla Bertelsen, Paola Piccini, David Brooks, Jorgen Alving, and Hans Lou. "Increased Dopamine Tone during Meditation- Induced Change of Consciousness." Cognitive Brain Research 13, no. 2 (April 2002)

Kölmel HW. 1985. Complex visual hallucinations in the hemianopic field. J Neurol Neurosurg Psychiatry.

Koenig, Harold. "Research on Religion, Spirituality, and Mental Health: A Review." Canadian Journal of Psychiatry 54, no. 5 (May 2009)

Koenig, Harold, ed. Handbook of Religion and Mental Health. San Diego, CA: Academic Press, 1998

Kraepelin E. Psychiatry: A Textbook for Students and Physicians. New York, NY: Science History Publications; 1990.

Lauglin, Charles, John McManus, and Eugene d'Aquili. Brain, Symbol, and

Experience. 2nd ed. New York: Columbia University Press, 1992

Lakoff, G. and M. Johnson (1999). Philosophy in the flesh. Basic Books: New York.

LeDoux, J. E. (1996). The emotional brain. New York: Simon & Schuster.

LeDoux, J.E. (1992), 'Emotion and the amygdala', in The Amygdala: Neurobiological Aspects of Emo- tion, Memory and Mental Dysfunction, ed J.P. Aggleton (New York: Wiley-Liss).

Levin, D.T. and Simons, D.J. (1997) Failure to detect changes to attended objects in motion pictures. Psychonomic Bulletin and Review 4, 501-6.

Levine,J. (1983) Materialism and qualia: the explanatory gap. Pacific Philosophical Quarterly 64, 354-61.

Levine,J. (2001) Purple Haze: The Puzzle of Consciousness. New York,

Oxford University Press. Levine, S. (1979) A Gradual Awakening. New York, Doubleday.

Levinson, B.W. (1965) States of awareness during general anaesthesia. British Journal of Anaesthesia 37, 544-6.

Lewicki, P., Czyzewska, M. and Hoffman, H. (1987) Unconscious acquisition of complex procedural knowledge. Journal of Experimental Psychology: Learning, Memory and Cognition 13, 523-30.

Lewicki, P., Hill, T. and Bizot, E. (1988) Acquisition of procedural knowledge about a pattern of stimuli that cannot be articulated. Cognitive Psychology 20, 24-37.

Lewicki, P., Hill, T. and Czyzewska, M. (1992) Nonconscious acquisition of information. American Psychologist 47, 796-801.

Manthey S, Schubotz RI, von Cramon DY (2003). Premotor cortex in observing erroneous action: an fMRI study. Brain Res Cogn Brain Res 15: 296–307.

Mesulam MM, Mufson EJ (1982) Insula of the old world monkey. III: Efferent cortical output and comments on function. J Comp Neurol 212: 38–52.

Naskar, Abhijit. "Homo: A Brief History of Consciousness", 2015

Naskar, Abhijit. "What is Mind?", 2016

Naskar, Abhijit. "In Search of Divinity: Journey to The Kingdom of Conscience", 2016

Naskar, Abhijit. "Love, God & Neurons: Memoir of A Scientist who found himself by getting lost", 2016

Naskar, Abhijit. "Neurons of Jesus: Mind of A Teacher, Spouse & Thinker", 2017

Naskar, Abhijit. "The Islamophobic Civilization: Voyage of Acceptance", 2017

Naskar, Abhijit. "Principia Humanitas", 2017

Naskar, Abhijit. "We Are All Black: A Treatise on Racism", 2017

Naskar, Abhijit. "Wise Mating: A Treatise on Monogamy", 2017

Naskar, Abhijit. "Either Civilized or Phobic: A Treatise on Homosexuality", 2017

Naskar, Abhijit. "Illusion of Religion: A Treatise on Religious Fundamentalism", 2017

Naskar, Abhijit. "I Am The Thread: My Mission", 2017

Naskar, Abhijit. "The Bengal Tigress: A Treatise on Gender Equality", 2017

Naskar, Abhijit. "Morality Absolute", 2017

Naskar, Abhijit. "Build Bridges not Walls: In the name of Americana", 2018

Naskar, Abhijit. "Fabric of Humanity", 2018

Naskar, Abhijit. "Lives To Serve Before I Sleep", 2019

Naskar, Abhijit. "Citizens of Peace: Beyond the Savagery of Sovereignty", 2019

Naskar, Abhijit. "The Constitution of The United Peoples of Earth", 2019

Naskar, Abhijit. "Neurons Giveth, Neurons Taketh Away | Abhijit Naskar | TEDxIIMRanchi", 2019 https://www.youtube.com/watch?v=BNX-Q0ySm80

Naskar, Abhijit. "Mission Reality", 2019

Naskar, Abhijit. "Operation Justice: To Make A Society That Needs No Law", 2019

Naskar, Abhijit. "Every Generation Needs Caretakers: The Gospel of Patriotism", 2020

Newberg, Andrew, and Jeremy Iversen. "The Neural Basis of the Complex Mental Task of Meditation: Neurotransmitter and Neurochemical Considerations." Medical Hypotheses 61, no. 2 (2003).

Newberg, Andrew. "How God Changes Your Brain: An Introduction to Jewish Neurotheology", CCAR Journal: The Reform Jewish Quarterly, Winter 2016.

Newberg, Andrew, and Stephanie Newberg. "A Neuropsychological Perspective on Spiritual Development." In Handbook of Spiritual Development in Childhood and Adolescence, edited by Eugene Roehlkepartain, Pamela King, Linda Wagener, and Peter Benson. London: Sage Publications, Inc., 2005

Newberg, Andrew. "The Neurotheology Link An Intersection Between Spirituality and Health", Alternative and Complimentary Therapies, Vol 21 No 1, February 2015.

Newberg, Andrew, Nancy Wintering, Dharma Khalsa, Hannah Roggenkamp, and Mark Waldman. "Meditation Effects on Cognitive Function and Cerebral Blood Flow in Subjects with Memory Loss: A Preliminary Study." Journal of Alzheimer's Disease 20, no. 2 (2010)

Nash, M. (1995), 'Glimpses of the mind', Time.

Nesse RM. Proximate and evolutionary studies of anxiety, stress and depression: synergy at the interface. Neurosci Biobehav Rev. 1999;23:895-903.

Nicolelis, Miguel. (2011) "Beyond Boundaries: The New Neuroscience of Connecting Brains with Machines---

and How It Will Change Our Lives", Times Books

O'Hara, K. and Scutt, T. (1996) There is no hard problem of consciousness. Journal of Consciousness Studies 3(4), 290-302, reprinted in J. Shear (ed.) (1997) Explaining Consciousness. Cambridge, MA, MIT Press, 69-82.

O'Regan, J.K. (1992) Solving the "real" mysteries of visual perception: the world as an outside memory. Canadian Journal of Psychology 46, 461-88.

O'Regan, J.K. and Noe, A. (2001) A sensorimotor account of vision and visual consciousness. Behavioral and Brain Sciences 24(5), 883-917.

O'Regan, J.K., Rensink, R.A. and Clark,].]. (1999) Change-blindness as a result of "mudsplashes." Nature 398, 34.

Ornstein, R.E. (1977) The Psychology of Consciousness (2nd edn). New York, Harcourt.

Ornstein, R.E. (1986) The Psychology of Consciousness (3rd edn). New York, Pehguin.

Ornstein, R.E. (1992) The Evolution of Consciousness. New York, Touchstone.

Penfield W, Faulk ME (1955) The insula: further observations on its function. Brain 78: 445– 470.

Penrose, R. (1994), Shadows of the Mind (Oxford: Oxford University Press).

Penrose, R. (1989), The Emperor's New Mind: Concerning Computers, Minds and The Laws of Physics (Oxford: Oxford University Press).

Persinger, "'I would kill in God's name' role of sex, weekly church attendance, report of a religious experience and limbic lability" Perceptual and Motor Skills 1997.

Persinger "Experimental simulation of the God experience" Neurotheology 2003.

Persinger, M. A. (1993b). Personality changes following brain injury as a grief response to the loss of sense of self: Phenomenological themes as indices of local lability and neurocognitive restructuring as psycho- therapy. Psychological Reports, 72

Persinger, Corradini, Clement, Keaney, et al "Neurotheology and its convergence with neuroquantology" NeuroQuantology 2010.

Persinger, Koren and St-Pierre "The electromagnetic induction of mystical and altered states within the laboratory" Journal of Consciousness Exploration and Research 2010.

Persinger "Case report: A prototypical spontaneous 'sensed presence' of a sentient being and concomitant electroencephalographic activity in the clinical laboratory" Neurocase 2008.

Persinger and Saroka "Potential production of Hughlings Jackson's "parasitic consciousness" by physiologically-patterned weak transcerebral magnetic fields: QEEG and source localization" Epilepsy & Behavior 28 (2013).

Persinger. "The neuropsychiatry of paranormal experiences". J Neuropsychiatry Clin Neurosci 2001.

Persinger. "Neuropsychological bases of god beliefs", New York: Praeger, 1987

Persinger. "Temporal lobe epileptic signs and correlative behaviors displayed by normal populations", Journal of General Psychology, 1986

Perry BD, Pollard R. Homeostasis, stress, trauma, and adaptation. A neurodevelopmental view of childhood trauma. Child Adolesc Psychiatr Clin N Am. 1998;7:33.

Paré, D. & Llinás, R. (1995), 'Conscious and preconscious processes as seen from the standpoint of sleep-waking cycle neurophysiology', Neuropsychologia, 33.

P. S. de Laplace. Essai Philosophique sur les Probabilites [1814], in Academy des Sciences, Oeuvres Complotes de Laplace, Vol. 7, Gauthier-Villars, Paris (1886).

Perrett DI, Harries MH, Bevan R, Thomas S, Benson PJ, Mistlin AJ, Chitty AJ, Hietanen JK, Ortega JE (1989) Frameworks of analysis for the neural representation of animate objects and actions. J Exp Bio 146: 87–113.

Phillips ML, Young AW, Senior C, Brammer M, Andrew C, Calder AJ, Bullmore ET, Perrett DI, Rowland D, Williams SC, Gray JA, David AS (1997) A specific neural substrate for perceiving facial expressions of disgust. Nature 389: 495–498.

Phillips ML, Young AW, Scott SK, Calder AJ, Andrew C, Giampietro V, Williams SC, Bullmore ET, Brammer M, Gray JA (1998) Neural responses to facial and vocal expressions of fear and disgust. Proc R Soc Lond B Biol Sci 265: 1809–1817.

Puce A, Perrett D (2003) Electrophysiological and brain imaging of biological motion. Philosoph Trans Royal Soc Lond, Series B, 358: 435–445.

Ramachandran VS. Behavioral and magnetoencephalographic correlates of plasticity in the adult human brain. Proc Natl Acad Sci USA 1993; 90: 10413–20.

Ramachandran VS. Phantom limbs, neglect syndromes, repressed memories, and Freudian psychology. Int Rev Neurobiol 1994; 37: 291–333.

Ramachandran VS. Plasticity and functional recovery in neurology. Clin Med 2005; 5: 368–73.

Ramachandran VS, Hirstein W. The perception of phantom limbs. The D. O. Hebb lecture. Brain 1998; 121: 1603–30.

Ramachandran VS, Rogers-Ramachandran D, Cobb S. Touching the phantom limb. Nature 1995; 377: 489–90.

Ramachandran VS, Rogers-Ramachandran D. Phantom limbs and neural plasticity. Arch Neurol 2000; 57: 317–20.

Ramachandran VS, Rogers-Ramachandran D. It's all done with mirrors. Sci Am Mind 2007; 18: 16–9.

Ramachandran VS, Rogers-Ramachandran D. Sensations referred to a patient's phantom arm from another subjects intact arm: perceptual correlates of mirror neurons. Med Hypotheses 2008; 70: 1233–4.

Ramachandran VS, Rogers-Ramachandran D, Stewart M. Perceptual correlates of massive cortical reorganization. Science 1992; 258: 1159–60.

Rizzolatti G, Craighero L (2004) The mirror-neuron system. Annu Rev Neurosci 27: 169–192.

Rizzolatti G, Fogassi L, Gallese V (2001) Neurophysiological mechanisms underlying the understanding and imitation of action. Nature Rev Neurosci 2:661–670.

Rock I, Victor J. Vision and touch: an experimentally created conflict between the two senses. Science 1964; 143: 594–6.

Rose´n B, Lundborg G. Training with a mirror in rehabilitation of the hand. Scand J Plast Reconstr Surg Hand Surg 2005; 39: 104–8.

Royet JP, Plailly J, Delon-Martin C, Kareken DA, Segebarth C (2003) fMRI of emotional responses to odors: influence of hedonic valence and judgment, handedness, and gender. Neuroimage 20: 713–728.

Rozin R Haidt J and McCauley CR (2000) Disgust. In: Lewis M, Haviland-Jones JM (eds) Handbook of Emotion. 2nd Edition. Guilford Press, New York, pp 637–653.

Saxe R, Carey S, Kanwisher N (2004) Understanding other minds: linking developmental psychology and functional neuroimaging. Annu Rev Psychol 55: 87–124.

S. J. Russell and P. Norvig, Artificial intelligence: a modern approach (3rd edition): Prentice Hall, 2009.

Schienle A, Stark R, Walter B, Blecker C, Ott U, Kirsch P, Sammer G, Vaitl D (2002) The insula is not specifically involved in disgust processing: an fMRI study. Neuroreport 13: 2023–2026.

Showers MJC, Lauer EW (1961) Somatovisceral motor patterns in the insula. J Comp Neurol 117: 107–115.

Singer T, Seymour B, O'Doherty J, Kaube H, Dolan RJ, Frith CD (2004) Empathy for pain involves the affective but not the sensory components of pain. Science 303: 1157–1162.

Smith A (1759) The theory of moral sentiments (ed. 1976). Clarendon Press, Oxford.

S. N. Bose (1924). "Plancks Gesetz und Lichtquantenhypothese". Zeitschrift für Physik. 26 (1): 178–181.

Sprengelmeyer R, Rausch M, Eysel UT, Przuntek H (1998) Neural structures associated with recognition of facial expressions of basic emotions Proc R Soc Lond B Biol Sci 265: 1927–1931.

Strafella AP, Paus T (2000) Modulation of cortical excitability during action observation: a transcranial magnetic stimulation study. NeuroReport 11: 2289–2292.

Simonsen R (2015) Eating for the future: veganism and the challenge of in vitro meat. In: Stapleton P, Byers A (Hg). Biopolitics and utopia. Palgrave Macmillan, New York (2015), S 167–190

Tanaka K (1996) Inferotemporal cortex and object vision. Ann Rev Neurosci. 19: 109–140.

Tesla N. "My Inventions", 1919

T. R. Society, "Machine learning: the power and promise of computers that learn by example," ed. The Royal Society, 2017.

Tomasello M, Call J (1997) Primate cognition. Oxford University Press, Oxford.

Tremblay C, Robert M, Pascual-Leone A, Lepore F, Nguyen DK, Carmant L, Bouthillier A, Theoret H (2004) Action observation and execution: intracranial recordings in a human subject. Neurology. 63: 937–938.

Umilta MA, Kohler E, Gallese V, Fogassi L, Fadiga L, Keysers C, Rizzolatti G (2001) "I know what you are doing": a neurophysiological study. Neuron 32: 91–101.

Von Wright G.H., (1963), Norm and Action. A Logical Inquiry, Routledge & Kegan Paul, London.

Von Wright G.H., (1976), "Determinism and the Study of Man", in Essays on Explanation and Understanding, ed. by J. Manninen and R. Tuomela, Reidel, Dordrecht.

Von Wright G.H., (1977), "What is Humanism?", The Lindlay Lecture, University of Arkansas, Lawrence, Kansas.

Von Wright G.H., (1979), "Humanism and the Humanities", in Philosophy and Grammar, ed. by S. Kanger and S. Öhman, Reidel, Dordrecht, pp. 1-16. Reprinted in von Wright (1993).

Von Wright G.H., (1980), Freedom and Determination, North-Holland Publishing Co., Amsterdam.

Von Wright G.H., (1985), Of Human Freedom, The Tanner Lectures on Human Values,

Vol. VI, ed. by S. M. McMurrin, University of Utah Press, Salt Lake City, pp. 107-70. Reprinted in von Wright (1998).

Von Wright G.H., (1993), The Tree of Knowledge and Other Essays, Brill, Leiden.

Von Wright G.H., (1997), "Progress: Fact and Fiction", in The Idea of Progress, ed. by A. Burgen et al., W. de Gruyter, Berlin, pp. 1-18.

Von Wright G.H., (1998), In the Shadow of Descartes: Essays in the Philosophy of Mind, Kluwer, Dordrecht.